YOU CAN'T CURL YOUR HAIR WITH HOLY ROLLERS

MICHAEL NOLAN & EVE SARRETT

A JANET THOMA BOOK

THOMAS NELSON PUBLISHERS
Nashville

Published in Nashville, Tennessee, by Janet Thoma Books, a division of Thomas Nelson, Inc., Publishers, and distributed in Canada by Word Communications, Ltd., Richmond, British Columbia, and in the United Kingdom by Word (UK), Ltd., Milton Keynes, England. Unless otherwise noted Scripture quotations are from the NEW KING JAMES VERSION of the Bible. Copyright © 1979, 1980, 1982, Nelson, Inc., Publishers.

Library of Congress Cataloging-in-Publication Data

Nolan, Mike, 1957–
    You can't curl your hair with holy rollers / by Mike Nolan, Eve Sarrett.
      p.   cm.
    "A Janet Thoma book."
    ISBN 0-8407-3444-1
    1. Fundamentalism—Humor. 2. Wit and humor—Religious aspects—Christianity.
  I. Sarrett, Eve. II. Title. III. Title: You cannot curl your hair with holy rollers.
BT82.2.N65   1993
202'.07—dc20
                                            93-2115
                                              CIP

Printed in the United States of America

1 2 3 4 5 6 - 98 97 96 95 94 93

DEDICATION

To the cheerleading section
of the Tuesday Night Dudes' Group
for laughing, crying, and changing my life.
—Michael

To the staff of Young Life,
past and present,
for how they have impacted my journey with Jesus
through laughter and love.
—Eve

ACKNOWLEDGMENTS

A great big thanks to the family members and friends who've encouraged and inspired us through the years. We salute all those diligent Sunday school teachers who turned flannelgraphs into an artform, the preachers who gave our minds the opportunity to both wonder and wander, and the youth workers who constantly reminded us that the Father must indeed have a terrific sense of humor. We are especially grateful to Janet, Susan, Laurie, Michelle, and the other folks at Team Thoma for having the nerve to put this idea into circulation.

Let us go down and confuse their language. Genesis 11:7

A funny thing happened on the way to the contemporary church—we began taking ourselves too seriously. Then we created our own little subculture with our own little churchspeak language that makes people outside the loop scratch their heads in disbelief. We utter something like "Do you have a quiet time?" and people around us wonder if we are speaking in tongues.

Our intention here is not to ridicule Christians—lots of people can do that better than us. Instead, we hope to remind readers that our call is to include those who need to hear the message of the cross rather than exclude those who don't have the gift of interpreting our phrases.

Of course, we hope you have a snicker, a chuckle, and maybe even a guffaw or two as you read this. Abraham laughed and God let him live so laughter must not be a sin. But we also hope this book makes you consider whether you've gotten so locked into Christian subculture that you confuse non-believers for all the wrong reasons.

Here's a little piety in your face.

Choose the appropriate meaning of these phrases:

Quiet time

    a. Period of laryngitis.

    b. The moment in Sunday school when the teacher asks for a volunteer to pray.

    c. Daily period one devotes to prayer and Bible study, which is used as a barometer for spirituality.

Profession of faith

a. Employment by the church or other God-related industry.

b. A earnest plea to God when it looks as if your car is destined for a head-on collision.

c. Nervous utterance of phrases recommended by your particular denomination which transform you from sinner to saint.

Parachurch organizations

a. A matched set of church organizations.

b. Clandestine wing of Christendom which relates to the church-at-large the way the paramilitary relates to the regular army.

c. Institutions that proclaim the Christian faith incognito without the benefit of stained glass, steeples, or (usually) funds.

Let's hold that up

    a. Let's plan an armed robbery.

    b. Let's create a traffic jam.

    c. Let's lift this prayer concern so it'll be easier for God to catch.

Lift up our pastor

   a. The precursor to singing "For He's a Jolly Good Fellow."

   b. Preparation for public hanging.

   c. Prayer that the pastor won't become like the last guy.

How's your walk?

a. Have you repaired your sidewalk?

b. Can you pass the Highway Patrol sobriety test?

c. Are you doing what you should and not what you shouldn't?

Anointed teaching

a. The orator has a good track record.

b. The teacher is saying things that I agree with and everyone else needs to hear.

c. We're packing 'em in so God must be blessing this pastor.

Share your heart

   a. Sign your organ donor card.

   b. Offer others a lick of your Valentine's candy.

   c. Tell us something hyperspiritual; or (in some cases)
   tell us the real dirt.

The event was under spiritual attack

    a. The event was poorly planned and executed.

    b. The event just didn't do anything for me.

    c. Everything went wrong so we're claiming Romans 8:37-39.

I have to pray about it.

a. I don't feel like telling you no right now.

b. I'm waiting to see what all my options are before committing.

c. I'm asking God to make the call on this one—if you disagree with the outcome, take it up with Him.

Forsaking the assembly of saints

a. Failing to attend the New Orleans pro football game.

b. Going fishing instead of going to church.

c. Your presence and tithe have been missed for several Sundays.

Blessed my socks off

a. Got yelled at.

b. Enjoyed attending a foot-washing service.

c. "Got so happy" that even the Pentecostals were asking me to chill out.

God laid it on my heart.

    a. A divine rebuke for eating spicy food.

    b. A gentler version of "laying it on the line."

    c. A spiritual way of saying, "I thought . . ."

The pastor accepted the call.

a. The minister footed the bill for someone phoning collect.

b. The minister didn't argue with the umpire.

c. The minister took advantage of getting out of his old church while the getting was good.

Desire of my heart

a. Title of latest Judith Krantz novel.

b. Lustful thoughts you want expurged through prayer.

c. Something you really, really, really want, usually with some spiritual significance: e.g., The desire of my heart is to begin a beach ministry in Hawaii.

Let's press in to worship.

a. Make room for the people who don't have seats.

b. Everyone run to the front of the sanctuary when I say go.

c. You need to get on the stick and praise God right.

Unspoken request

a. A mime's expression of his needs.

b. What you want to say but don't: e.g., "Take that crying baby out of the sanctuary."

c. A desire for prayer about something too juicy to trust to your fellow parishioners, which allows them an opportunity to use their imaginations.

Name it and claim it.

a. New game show hosted by Alex Trebek.

b. Spiritual jargon for church's lost and found area.

c. A way to give God your wish list, with the expectation that His will is to bring about your will.

Altar call

    a. Brand name of a pulpit phone.

    b. Another name to describe a pastor search.

    c. The time during the service when those unsure of their salvation start sweating and the saved know the end of the service is in sight.

YOU ARE CHURCHED BEYOND  IF . . .

It bugs you when someone sits in "your" pew.

You know all 155 variations of potato salad.

You're able to recite the ABC's of salvation, 4 spiritual laws, 5 steps to freedom in Christ, 9 fruits of the Spirit, and 12 spiritual gifts.

You have a customized Bible cover.

You remember when the New American Standard Version and New International Version were really new.

You keep a separate calendar for all your church committee meetings.

"Praise-and-worship" has become a single word.

You can turn pages of your Bible pages without making those crinkling noises.

You methodically use a variety of highlighter colors to mark your Bible.

The name of your church includes all three persons of the Trinity.

You can quote more from Bill Gothard than the apostle Paul.

The only verb you can think of which means "to express oneself" is *share*.

You add a closet exclusively to store Easter hats.

You know the hymns by the numbers.

You attended Walk Thru the Bible, Emmaus Road, and
Marriage Encounter Weekend in a single year.

The outgoing message on your answering machine includes a
Bible verse.

More than one of your children is named after a minor
prophet.

Children, live animals, straw, and torches are a combustible combination.

Most Wal-Marts don't carry myrrh.

You must watch your step around nervous farm animals.

No one wants to play the innkeeper.

Church pyromaniacs fight to rig Star of Bethlehem.

Unchurched kids come to look for gold, Frankenstein, and Merv.

Shoving matches break out between new mothers over whose baby gets to play the Christ-child.

Camels can spit.

Feminists protest use of three wise *men*.

Icy northern winds cut through those white sheets worn by
angels.

FASHION AND : A STUDY FROM THE OUTSIDE IN

Although looks may be deceiving, they may be enlightening as well.

Sackcloth and Laura Ashley

At the church for dignified yuppies the fashion philosophy is this: If you were going to see a judge, you'd want to look your best; at church, you're going to see The Judge of All Creation, so you'd better look spiffy. (Of course, dressing well isn't everything—you also have to make sure your kids go to the right schools, preferably a Christian academy.)

You'll find more jumpers here than at a steeplechase —all *very* tasteful. For these floral-frocked folks, the "prints of peace" takes on a whole new meaning.

The Tribe of Levis

Convinced that jeans fade but hope doesn't, these people firmly believe "there is now no con*denim*nation for those who are in Christ Jesus." They'd rather be associated with acid-washed jeans than whitewashed tombs. In most of their assemblies, John the Baptist in his camel's hair and leather belt would go completely unnoticed.

To complement their dungarees, these faithful followers often wear born-again T-shirts, both those of the latest Christian artists and those inscribed with messages like "The world has fallen and it can't get up" (Romans 3:23).

Liz ClaiborneAgain/Bill Bless

Generally found at historically significant churches, these parishioners just wouldn't feel as if they had attended church if they weren't dressed for the occasion. They rally around the thought: "Consider the Lilli Rubensteins . . . Solomon in all his glory was not arrayed as one of these." But they note Solomon probably would have done better had he had access to a good stock of silk or Pendleton wool.

Rejoicing in that old favorite, "Crown them with many hats," the ladies in these churches know how to accessorize. For them, Jesus' parables about sowing seeds or finding sheep don't mean much. But selling all to buy the pearl of great value, now there's a story.

Casual Christians

Perhaps birthed in Southern California, these easy-going people believe that God wants us to be comfortable in His presence, preferably by wearing Dockers and knit shirts. When studying the gap that separated the rich man and Lazarus, most picture a store in the mall between Benetton and Eddie Bauer. As the kids in children's church learn about Joseph's coat of many colors, they ask if it was from the Alexander Julian collection.

K-Martyrs

These salt-of-the-earth followers tend to live conservatively, think conservatively, and believe conservatively. They don't see spending a lot of money on apparel; in fact, they often quote Luke 12:23: "Life is more than food, and the body more than clothes."

Aside from perhaps going a little crazy in the hair accessories department, they really aren't interested in investing hard-earned money on the latest fashions. That's why they're able to buy satellite dishes, radar detectors, and tracer lights for their "God is My Co-Pilot" license plates.

BIBLE STORIES DELETED BECAUSE THEY WERE CONSIDERED UNINSPIRED

Children of Israel throw paper wads at Gibeonites until someone puts an eye out.

Jezebel meets the Hardy Boys.

Two guys smother when God throws open the storehouses of heaven.

Joshua leads the children of Israel to Gilligan's Island.

Elijah wins the Boston Marathon.

Isaac steps on a crack and breaks his mother's back.

Lot's sister-in-law looks back and is turned into pepper.

Rahab talks to the tabloid newspaper reporter.

Lifeguards in Pharaoh's army executed.

Lazarus tries to explain resurrection to his life insurance agent.

David gets a song publishing deal.

Moses prays for the vegetarians and zucchini falls from heaven.

 FOR THE 21st CENTURY

Joan of Golden Arcs

Sustainer of the McDonald's that youth groups visit

St. Joseph

Supplier of aspirin

St. Paul Simon

Giver of lyrics to world beat songs

St. Sealy Serta

Atoner for those who remove mattress tags

St. Litton of Amana

Protector of those who put metal in their microwave ovens

St. Wire the Less

Guardian of lost remote controls

St. Earl of Olay

Protector of youthful physical appearance

St. August Cliché'

Giver of lyrics to gospel songwriters

St. Muffy

Shielder of stains from tennis dresses

St. Never Mary

Comforter of career singles

St. Louie Louie

Revitalizer of golden oldies

St. Elmos Friar

Pamperer of brooding yuppies

St. Laurent

Inspirer of stylish fashion

HOW TO STIR UP A CONGREGATION

Depending on your denomination, there are magical phrases you can evoke to get your church fired up.

AME Church: Isn't the Lord Jesus good?

Pentecostal Church: Satan, we bind you from this place.

Holiness Church: We seem to be missing a snake up here.

Catholic Church:	The mass is ended. Go in peace. Thanks be to God.
Unitarian Church:	Let's start a recycling program.
Baptist Church:	Let's build something.
Episcopal Church:	Someone backed into a Mercedes in the parking lot.

LET THERE BE LIGHTBULB JOKES

How many Southern Baptists does it take to change a lightbulb?

15,738,283 (at last count), but they can't agree if it really needs to be changed.

How many campfire worship leaders does it take to change a lightbulb?

One. But soon all those around can warm up in its glowing.

How many Mennonites does it take to change a lightbulb?

Eventually about five, but they can get along fine without it.

How many televangelists does it take to change a lightbulb?

Only one, but for the message of change to continue to go forth, send in your check today.

How many Mormon missionaries does it take to change a lightbulb?

Two. One to bike over to the hardware store and one to do it.

How many Episcopalians does it take to change a lightbulb?

Three. One to do it, one to bless the element, and one to pour the sherry.

How many Nazarenes does it take to change a lightbulb?

Eleven. One to change it and ten to organize the fellowship supper that follows.

How many Presbyterians does it take to change a lightbulb?

They're not sure, but there's a committee studying the issue.

How many Amish does it take to change a lightbulb?

What's a lightbulb?

How many members of the Church of Christ does it take to change a lightbulb?

Only one, but if anyone else tries to do it, the light won't come on.

How many Methodists does it take to change a lightbulb?

Only one, but first they want to make sure no one is offended by the change.

How many Catholics does it take to change a lightbulb?

Nine. One to change it and eight to sell raffle tickets on the old one.

How many charismatics does it take to change a lightbulb?

Three. One to do it and two to bind the spirit of darkness.

How many Jehovah's Witnesses does it take to change a lightbulb?

It doesn't matter because you won't let them in to change it anyway.

Sonny and Cher reunion tour

Turn left from right lane only

Mimes elected to political office

PTL wavepool divides for youth group to cross on dry land

Horrormaster Clive Barker seems like a pretty well-adjusted
   guy

Snooze buttons on clock radios required by law to
administer mild electric charges

Cable introduces the All-Disaster Channel

Parking spaces grow narrower

"Sally Jessy Raphael" expands to 90 minutes

McDonald's sign reads "Over 666 Million Served"

Mr. Rogers jailed for being too nice

Attention spans so decreased you can't even finish a

NEW IDEAS TO ATTRACT THE

David Copperfield recreates the ten plagues of Egypt

"Motown Salutes the Women of the Bible"

Deacons limbo for opening processional

Blessing of completed tax returns

Cliff diving into baptistry

Tithe-Lotto

Story of Samson told using clips from Rambo movies

Business card swap during fellowship coffee

Service which combines born-again experiences and beauty
   makeovers

Super Bowl party with prayers at halftime

Life of Christ told using Elvis' songs including "My Way,"
"Love Me Tender," and "Don't Be Cruel"

Live walk-through recreation of Sodom and Gomorrah

Bungee-cord leaps of faith

Methodists introduce "Calvinist and Hobbes" cartoon strip

HOW TO MAKE A HOSPITAL VISIT

Showing concern for the sick and afflicted of your church is as central to the Christian faith as referring to them in public prayers as "the sick and afflicted." Of course, such terminology probably doesn't help their recovery, but it sounds spiritual. Since praying for the sick is pretty much confined to the faith department, you need to augment your concern for them with works, i.e., a hospital visit.

Plan this benevolent act to occur outside of regular visiting hours. This affords you a better parking space (assuming the pastor spaces are already taken) and allows you to avoid other people from your church who bother you.

Take someone with you in case the patient is not feeling up to talking and you need a conversation partner. On your way through the hospital lobby, consider stopping at the gift shop and buying something until you remember how overpriced everything there is.

After getting lost several times because "people just don't know how to give directions," arrive at the correct room. Enter timidly with a deceptively soft knock, followed by quoting Revelation 3:20, "Behold! I stand at the door and knock." Don't worry if the patient is asleep or unprepared for visitors—your arrival should be considered "a nice surprise."

Assuming your best bedside manner, look deeply into the patient's eyes and ask, "How are you feeling?" Listen sympathetically to the response. Nod your head and respond, "Oh, I know how awful this is for you." Then relate a story of someone you know who had the same problem but experienced horrendous complications (possibly due to a lack of faith). Allow your pastor visitor cohort to interrupt by interjecting, "Of course, that's not going to happen to you," and change the subject to a) the view from the window, b) who sent flowers, or c) the blandness of hospital food.

Without any solicitation for help from your friend, plump the pillows, raise or lower the bed, open or close the curtains, and busy yourself about, making the room neat. Don't mind the protests of your friend.

Look at your watch and realize your favorite television show is about to come on. Ask, "You don't mind if I watch my program, do you?" Change the TV channel, and make sure the volume is loud enough so you can still hear it as you carry on a conversation.

All that talk will make you thirsty, so feel free to ask if you could have one of those little cans of juice from a recently delivered fruit basket. Remain calm as you struggle to tear the cellophane and then realize, after you reach inside, that the florist has taped everything together, thus creating a festive boobytrap of fruit, cans, bottles, and plastic grass.

As a guest, feel free also to pick your way through the box of chocolates. If needed, poke the underside of the candies to make sure you don't get any undesirably flavored centers.

If the patient is in a semi-private room, half-whisper, "What is that person in for?" Depending on the response, blanch, wince, or raise an eyebrow. Ask, "Does he/she know the

Lord?" if the answer is yes, initiate a conversation of spiritual one-upsmanship—who's got the largest membership, biggest building, best pastor, or most ministry projects. If the person is not known to be a Christian, offer to bring your friend sermon tapes, which can be played loudly enough for the other patient to hear and possibly come under conviction.

Stay until the nurse shoos you out, noting that you don't know why nurses have to be so bossy. Use this opportunity to voice your views on the health care industry, portraying doctors as inaccessible know-it-alls and hospitals as Medicare vultures.

Look back at your friend and say, "Well, I guess we'd better be going," as you dust yourself for food crumbs. Take the patient's hand and ask, "Is there anything we can do for you before we go?" When the anticipated no is uttered, tell the patient you expect a call if he/she needs anything, knowing/hoping this won't happen ever. Note the emotional response illicited from the patient when you say that you'll come back and visit again in a day or two.

"Bless Me Big" Bible—

Created for the children of those who revel in prosperity doctrine. For example, to make sure kids get the message, the word *toys* replaces *joy* to create really exciting verses: "But the angel said to them, 'Do not be afraid. I bring you good news of great toys that will be for all the people' " (Luke 2:10).

"Word to Your Mother" Rapper's Bible—

Takes the gospel with a beat to the boyz on the street
and comes as a shock to the new kids on the block.
Busts loose with the Word straight up like, "It'd be cool
if'n you was smokin' or chillin' but 'cause you ain't got
the juice, you're gonna get chucked" (Revelation 3:16).

Con Version of the Bible—

Pioneered by Chuck Colson, this translation includes highlighted passages that refer to jails, prisons, and shackles. It has been officially endorsed by a growing number of churches who embrace the concept of "cell groups."

The "Isn't That In The Bible" Bible—
   Includes all the pithy sayings that aren't really scripture
   but sound as if they ought to be. Featured verses include
      "God helps those who help themselves."
      "God works in mysterious ways."
      "Cleanliness is next to godliness."
      "You can't get to heaven on the end of a kite."

Inn Version—

Placed in motels and hotels across the world, the Inn Version features a full-color illustration of Joseph and Mary in front of a No Vacancy sign in Bethlehem. Special commentary draws parallels between the five wise virgins who had extra oil for their lamps and Motel 6 managers who "leave the light on."

Aversion Version—

If you really don't want to have anything to do with Christianity but you know your godly little grandmother is going to give you a Bible for Christmas or your birthday anyway, request the AV. The Aversion Version highlights conviction-free verses, including "let us love one another" (1 John 4:7a) and "practice hospitality" (Romans 12:13b).

SPIRITUAL GIFTS PAUL FORGOT TO MENTION

Never missing Sunday school

Discerning whether the recitation of "The Lord's Prayer" will
use the word *debts* or *trespasses*

Taking communion while balancing a two year old on your
lap

Remembering to take your Bible to Bible study

Making gravy

Pronouncing *propitiation*

Reciting all 66 books of the Bible in order

Teaching junior high Sunday school alone

Finding a verse in the book of Obadiah

Pew jumping

Saying aloud "Lord, we pray" three times without it sounding like "Lord, we play"

Matchmaking singles

Unlocking a car door with a coathanger

Interpreting your baby's prayer language

Finding a parking space near the front door

Anticipating the pastor's planned pause and saying amen
    right on cue

Making kitchen plastic wrap stick

Balancing a Bible on the back of the pew in front of you

Finding the book of Nahum

Finding hidden microphone in church bathroom connected to auditorium public address system

Dumping communion tray in lap

Realizing you're not wearing anything beneath your choir robe

Coming down with a case of "TV evangelist" hair

Belting out verse 2 of the hymn when everyone else skips to verse 3

Having to read aloud the "begat" section of Matthew 1

Spirit-filled member of congregation receiving a word of
    knowledge and revealing your "unspoken" prayer request

Being jolted from daydream and called upon to pray for
    someone's heartfelt need

Rapture happening and you're left behind still watching
    "American Gladiators"

Come directly to the restaurant from a church gathering, with a large number of people—preferably too many to sit at one table.

Bring as many children with you as possible, especially whiny babies and strong-willed toddlers who have been forced to be quiet for the past two hours and will need to be loudly corrected. Ask to be seated together, saying, "We don't mind scrunching a little." Remember to complain later about how crowded you were at the table they gave you.

When you arrive at your table, someone should inadvertently bring a Bible with him, which will take up much-needed table space. When the hostess asks if you prefer smoking or non-smoking, look appalled and cite how smoking defiles the temple of God. Act as confused as possible about who sits where. Several people should swap seats a few times, especially after orders have been placed. When the server arrives, request as many separate checks as possible, or use zigzag patterns to indicate who should be included on a single check. At least one person should request only water and say to the server, "I'm just here for the fellowship." This person must consume as much water as possible, requiring multiple refills, and should scarf food from the plates of those who order the all-you-can-eat salad bar.

When the food comes, reel off a long, confusing list of orders that are wrong and items that have been forgotten. The meals in place, join others in nervously looking around the table until someone asks what everyone is thinking: "Are we going to pray?" Wait the long, tenuous moment until someone surrenders and responds, "I'll do it." Fumble with the hold-hands/not-hold-hands decision and bow your heads just as server arrives with a heavy tray of additional stuff. Have a long prayer, including in it a brief summation of the sermon and a spirited call to action. Keep praying until waiter or waitress develops muscle spasms.

Young children should crush as many crackers as possible. When a toddler stands in his chair and refuses to sit down, the parent should say, "Santa Claus won't come to see you if you keep this up" or, "When you act this way, you make God cry." Eventually, the parent should drag the kicking-and-screaming child to the bathroom, while spanking the young reprobate and reciting Ephesians 6:1.

When the checks are distributed, several people should find errors and complain loudly. Those who have not been charged for items they received should offer a silent prayer to God for His abundant provision. Each person should tip 5

percent or however many coins they have in their pockets—
whichever is less. Someone should remember that change is
needed to buy a newspaper and take the appropriate
amount. Place coins under plates, believing that all giving—
not just tithing—should be done in secret.

Finally, someone should leave a card with the tip,
quoting Luke 9:25, "What does it profit a man if he gaineth
the world yet loseth his own soul?" or Joshua 24:15,
"Choose ye this day whom ye will serve.'

THE CONSECRATED CONSUMER

How many of the following items are you blessed with?

Personalized license plate with spiritual significance

"As for me and my house, we will serve the Lord" door knocker

More than one scripture in needlepoint

Free gift book from a television ministry that you've never read

Scrapbook cataloging all back issues of church bulletin

Anything written by Dale Evans

Painting of Jesus sitting in an office

Entire drawer of bedroom dresser devoted to shirts with Christian messages

Both covers of Amy Grant's first album or all four versions of her "Unguarded" album

Workbooks from more than five conferences (that you really plan to finish filling out someday)

Eagle statuary or plaques which quote Isaiah 40:31

Checks printed with Scripture or fish

Church attendance badges or certificates

Certificate or placard which tells what family members' names mean in Greek or Hebrew

Items which feature the poem "Footprints"

LITTLE-KNOWN  FACTIONS

Prehistoric Baptist—predates Primitive Baptist by several millennia

Third Baptist to the Fifth Power—totals to create 243rd Baptist

Sam's Baptist—controversial joint venture of Wal-Mart and Baptist Church which guarantees members a ten percent savings on tithe dollars

Original and Extra Crispy Baptist—believes that hell is even hotter than hell

Buddhist Baptist—adheres to the doctrine of "once shaved, always shaved"

AAA Baptist—just a clever marketing ploy to be the first Baptist Church in Yellow Page listings

Rehabtist—offers a 17-step program which includes AA's 12-steps plus Baptists' 5-steps to salvation

McBaptist—home of the golden crosses with over 1 million saved, known for singing updated hymns such as "McLeaning on Jesus"

MacBaptist—though sometimes confused with McBaptists, these computer-age believers refer to "born-again experiences" as being "reformatted for eternity"

Your Sunday school teacher didn't prepare when

    a. announcements or prayer time lasts the entire period.

    b. he/she suggests that the class needs to break down barriers and whips out the game of Twister.

    c. he/she says, "Hey, how long's it been since you've had a Sword drill?"

The church is running behind in contributions when

a. the pastor preaches from Malachi 3:8, asking the "cost-ic" question, Will a man rob God?

b. the children's sermon includes a plug for tithing.

c. the church bulletin comes postage-due.

The baptistry is cold when

    a. candidates for baptism are first immersed in Vaseline.

    b. the cause of "death to the 'old man' of sin" is hypothermia.

    c. the preacher has a loop on his hip waders for an ice ax.

HEART OF HEARTS
93

The youth fundraiser was a bust when

a. the youth pastor claims Philippians 3:8, "I count it all loss."

b. the bank puts a lien on the youth group's Michael W. Smith tapes.

c. a new fundraising effort is started to pay for the last one.

The missions trip was hard when

a. the pastor asks for all the survivors to stand.

b. next year's missions budget will be used to pay for counseling for this year's missions participants.

c. someone reads Paul's hardships in 2 Corinthians 11 and the missions team members caustically mutter, "Big deal! What a wimp!"

SURE SIGNS THAT THE SERVICE HAS RUN LONG

Older men in the congregation wake up from their naps refreshed and ready for lunch.

Deacons' ties come back into style.

Baptistry water has evaporated.

Pastor's wife dozes off.

Widows break out their knitting.

People fake coughing fits in order to leave auditorium.

You have counted all of the light fixtures, ceiling tiles, or
pews in the sanctuary to pass time.

Leviticus seems intriguing.

The youth group has exhausted supply of visitation cards and
offering envelopes for note-writing.

Communion does not "tide you over" till lunch.

Tribulation and the sermon seem somewhat synonymous.

New Englanders give precise directions.

Deluded millions pattern their lives after the wit and wisdom of Jean Claude Van Damme.

Square pegs fit in round holes.

Wile E. Coyote catches the Road Runner.

"Based on a true story" TV movies are filmed before the real event has taken place.

Aerobics found to cause cancer in lab mice.

TV weathermen seem a little moody.

"Three's Company" rejoins primetime line-up.

Shop clerks' farewell becomes "Have a wretched day."

Baskin-Robbins introduces new flavor: toxic waste ripple.

Christians are main course at new Lion Country Safari
feeding exhibit.

Everyone is required to wear powder blue eyeshadow.

Premiere of Disney sequel: *Honey, I Tattooed the Kids with
666's.*

Codependency

> I have made a fool of myself, but you drove me to it.
>
> *2 Corinthians 12:11a (NIV)*

Dancing

> Let us keep in step with the Spirit.
>
> *Galatians 5:25b (NIV)*

Repossession

> Your very bed will be snatched from under you.
>
> *Proverbs 22:27b (NIV)*

Television evangelist's appeals for money

> The leech has two daughters. "Give! Give!" they cry.
>
> *Proverbs 30:15a (NIV)*

Napping during church services

(God) grants sleep to those he loves.

Psalm 127:2b (NIV)

Insomnia

Blessed is he who stays awake.

Revelation 16:15b (NIV)

Dieting

"May God deal with me, be it ever so severely, if I taste bread or anything else before the sun sets!"

2 Samuel 3:35b (NIV)

Dieting, the sequel

Set a guard over my mouth, O Lord; keep watch over the doors of my lips.

Psalm 141:3 (NIV)

Vegetarianism

You . . . have need of milk and not of strong meat.

Hebrews 5:12b (KJV)

Blind ambition

I can testify that, if you could have done so, you would have torn out your eyes and given them to me.

Galatians 4:15 (NIV)

Dating services

Catch for us the foxes.

Song of Solomon 2:15a (NIV)

Being gullible

They took the bull given them.

1 Kings 18:26a (NIV)

YOU HAVE A SPIRIT OF  IF YOU. . .

Peek when the pastor asks for "every head bowed, every eye closed."

Sign your name illegibly on weekly membership cards to frustrate church secretary.

Interrupt the pastor's sermon to ask how much money he makes.

Refuse to join a church you've been faithfully attending for seventeen years.

Move the Reserved: Pastor parking sign to the far side of the building.

Fill out a building fund pledge card for a huge amount of money and sign someone else's name.

Drag the hymnal from the songbook rack *before* the preacher heads for the sermon closing.

Create mystery hunt in hymnal by writing "Turn to" on random pages.

Fake yawning during the sermon to make others yawn.

Switch the signs on men's and women's restrooms.

Write captions beneath photos in church pictorial directory.

Wonder if you could get away with taking money out of the offering basket.

Slip wedding announcements of terminally single friends into church bulletin.

Spray offering plates with WD-40.

DARING ALTERNATE MELODIES FOR AMAZING GRACE

"I'd Like to Teach the World to Sing"

"Blowin' in the Wind"

"Peaceful Easy Feeling"

"House of the Rising Sun"

"The Star Spangled Banner"

"Ice, Ice Baby"

"Windy"

"Joy to the World"

"Theme from 'Gilligan's Island'"

"On the Road Again"

"Theme from 'The Brady Bunch'"

"Hey Jude"

"I Wish They All Could Be California Girls"

We put the *fun* back into fundamentalism

Come hear the faster pastor

A prize in every offering envelope—guaranteed

Snakes—never had 'em, never will

Tonight only: city council members take their licks on our
baptistry dunking machine

Come see if the rumors are true

Tonight the choir goes robeless—come if you dare

Play the Mystery Usher Game

Class up your resumé by putting your name on our church
roll

Try to suppress laughter by bowing your head, holding your breath, and biting your lip. Close your eyes. Try in vain to think of sad things. As the hilarity builds, think over and over again, *I'm not going to laugh. I'm not going to laugh.* Make little snorting sounds. Tighten your stomach muscles. Let your shoulders shake. Sense that you are making the whole pew vibrate. Do everything in your power to stop these convulsions.

Sneak a look at your pewmates, hoping to see if they're cracking up. They will be doing the same, thus intensifying the desire to laugh. Feel the stares of the crankiest people

in the church. Realize that their stares only make things worse.

Continue to hold your breath. Think about trying to make a break for the door but fear that you'll never make it.

By now, tears will be welling up in your eyes. If you go to a charismatic church, people will assume that the Holy Spirit is at work in your life to bring about healing from some long-suppressed emotional trauma. Compassionate people will gather around you to pray. Accept that you have no choice but to go along with this.

As minutes pass, the wave of hilarity will give way to a sense of embarrassment. Thank the people who prayed for you. Look over at your co-conspirators and shake head in mock-shame.

Wiggle your eyebrows and slip them a sly grin.

NAMES  YOU'D NEVER GIVE YOUR CHILDREN

Ocran	Puah
Beor	Zadok
Ard	Guni
Zuar	Mushi
Og	Er
Huz	Bildad
Buz	Ehud

Nuzi	Boaz
Obed	Uzziah
Jezebel	Joda
Izhar	Nahor
Jezer	Judas
Enos	Onan
Gad	Herod
Igal	Doeg the Edomite

CHAPTERS PARENTS WANT TO ADD TO 'S *Dare to Discipline*

"I'm Your Mother, That's Why"

"The Rack: An Old-Fashioned Way to Really Stretch Your Child"

"Because I Said So"

"Do It Again and I'm Selling You to Gypsies"

"Just Try Me"

"Rooted . . . And Grounded (in Love)"

"Stay in Your Womb: Disciplining the Unborn"

"Subliminal Suggestion: How Whispering Threats in Your
Child's Ear During Naptime Can Improve Behavior"

"Don't Make Me Have to Come in There Again"

"Forcing Kids to Go to Youth Group So the Youth Pastor Can
Deal with Them"

"This Is Your Very Last Final Warning. Do Your Hear Me?"

"Choosing the Right Military School for Your Child"

LEADING GRIPES OF CHILDREN IN SUNDAY SCHOOL

With all the yummy snacks in the world, whose bright idea was graham crackers?

The rewards for playing "Quiet Mouse" are not very good.

Bag those gold stars for perfect attendance; replace them with Toys'R'Us gift certificates.

End our confusion: Were there or weren't there two Ninja Turtles on the ark?

We need hipper choreography for hand-motion songs.

Read my lips: no plastic scissors.

The production values in puppet shows are weak.

Why can't we get paste in better flavors?

Before you get out of your car to go into the garage, be sure to strew witnessing tracts throughout car interior and make sure the radio is set on a Christian station because you never know when you might plant a seed of faith.

Enter the shop saying you don't normally patronize pagans but your regular Christian mechanic got mad because your last check bounced. Mention that your previous serviceman also got hacked because you wanted him to tell you what to do to fix your car yourself and then asked to borrow his tools. Say you don't know what this world is coming to.

Suggest that your mechanical problems may be a demonic attack because you use the car for Meals-on-

Wheels, to visit shut-ins, and go on road trips with the church league ball team. When the mechanic goes out to inspect your car, follow him, and look over his shoulder saying, "It's not that I don't trust you but you know how people in your profession are."

When the mechanic invites you to have a seat while he figures up the estimate, take out a handkerchief and wipe the chair before sitting. Tell him that you hope this bill won't cut too deeply into your tithe. Nervously chit-chat about his business. Use ethnic slurs to refer to the makers of imported cars. Under your breath, rebuke his auto-parts calendar, which features pictures of girls in swimsuits.

When he shows you the estimate, ask if he's sure he added things correctly. Say, "Well, it looks like you've got me over a barrel here." Inquire about when the work will be completed, reminding him, "You know how most mechanics are. Your car is never ready when they say."

Sign off on the work and mention that you want to make one last check of your car to make sure you aren't leaving anything valuable because "things just seem to walk away at these garages." After collecting all your belongings, wait for a friend to pick you up. When he or she arrives, thank them for coming and say how happy you'll be when you're all in heaven where there won't be any carburetors or flywheels.

STEPHEN KING FAVORITE BIBLE STORIES

Man has six fingers on each hand and six toes on each foot
   (2 Samuel 21:20)

Twelve plagues of Egypt (Exodus 7-11)

Nebuchadnezzar given the mind of an animal (Daniel 5:21)

Burning sulphur rains down on Sodom and Gomorrah
   (Genesis 19)

God hurls huge hailstones to kill Israelites' enemies (Joshua 10:11)

Obese king stabbed; fat closes in around sword (Judges 3:21-22)

Samson kills a thousand Philistines with a donkey's jawbone (Judges 15:15)

Demons cause mass suicide of pigs (Mark 5:13)

Dream of seven scrawny, ugly cows eating seven fat, healthy
   cows (Genesis 41:17-21)

Egyptian army fails flotation test in Red Sea (Exodus 14)

Joseph's brothers throw him in a well—although the story
   would've been better if there had been leeches in the
   well (Genesis 37:24)

Seminaries become hotbed for genuine faith

All-State introduces brimstone insurance with really high
premiums

Fewer vowels included in the game of Scrabble

Spitting into wind becomes Olympic event

Sluggo and Nancy reveal neo-Nazi ties

Possible to lead a horse to water and make him drink

Zombies attain minority status

$a^2 + b^2$ no longer equals c^2

Televangelists donate big bucks to reduce national debt

VCRs discipline children they're
babysitting

Disturbing number of friends work in
telephone sales

The release of *Home Alone 7* finds
Kevin lost in eternity

The fat lady sings

Whale of a mess

Jonah, speaking from somewhere near blowhole

I need this like I need a hole in the head.

Goliath to Philistine buddies

You've got rocks for brains.

David to Goliath, soon after giving his sling a fling

You think you've got trouble?!

Job to anyone who would listen

Take my wives—please.

Solomon to court jester

It all comes out in the wash.

Naaman to soon-to-be former leper

This place is an absolute zoo.

Mrs. Noah to Noah in the ark, Day 137

Oh yeah? You and what army?

Gibeonites to Israelites just prior to God throwing hailstones

What are you, a wise guy?

Herod to a visitor from the East

Is it hot in here or it is just me?

Shadrach to Meshach and Abednego

Well, this is just the pits!

Joseph to himself after telling his brothers about one too many dreams

Man, I'm having a bad hair day!

Samson to himself after Delilah gave him a buzz cut

To get modern heathens to wake up and smell the coffee, try these updated metaphors for what eternity in hell would be like.

Experiencing an eternal IRS audit

Watching an endless slow-motion video of a BMW being
    scratched

Being only chaperone on a junior high field trip

Finding your cable TV stuck on The Weather Channel

Sitting through every graduation ceremony on Planet Earth

Listening to one 12-year-old teach another to play "Chopsticks"

Becoming a porkchop, and the devil is a pit bull

Neighborhood blabbermouth learning the number of your cellular phone

Living above a bowling alley

Having to do telephone solicitation for a dance studio

The casseroles John the Baptist brought to covered dish dinners frequently made people queasy.

It was really hard to keep your sandals clean in the land that flowed with milk and honey.

Methuselah used to cut line, saying, "Age before beauty."

A popular joke in the Promised Land was, "So you're from Ai. How do you spell that?"

For kicks, Hannah and Eve liked to spell their names backwards.

The name Malachi does not rhyme with hibachi.

The TV show "Mr. Ed" was inspired by the story of Balaam's donkey.

Church offerings increased tremendously after the untimely deaths of Ananias and Sapphira.

"Pharoah-row-row-your-boat" was a popular Egyptian slave song.

It is easier for a camel to pass through the eye of a needle than a rich man to enter into heaven. (Matthew 10:25)

It is easier to

    explain Monty Python's humor to your parents

    get your order right at a restaurant drive-thru

    assemble a bicycle

    program a VCR

It would be better for him to be thrown into the sea with a millstone tied around his neck than for him to cause one of these little ones to sin. (Luke 17:2)

It would be better for him to

    stand in the grocery express lane with 13 items

    wear a fur coat to an animal rights activists' rally

    say Hank Williams, Jr. is a sissy in a country bar

(The ordinances of the Lord) are more desirable than much fine gold. (Psalm 19:10)

They are more desirable than
a percentage of *Home Alone*'s profits
fat-free hot fudge sundaes
Jack Nicholson's seats at Lakers' games
a good hair day

I will surely bless you and make your descendants as numerous as the stars in the sky and as the sand on the seashore. (Genesis 22:17) NIV

I will . . . make your descendants as numerous as
    tied-dyed T-shirts at a Grateful Dead concert
    liberals in Hollywood
    lawyers in Washington
    college students in Daytona on spring break

Some trust in chariots and some in horses, but we trust in the name of the Lord our God. (Psalm 20:7) NIV

Some trust in
> Republicans and some in Democrats
> IRAs and some trust in Keoghs
> aspirin and some trust in ibuprofen
> Siskel and some in Ebert

If anyone causes one of these little ones who believe in me to sin, it would be better for him to have a large millstone hung around his neck and to be drowned in the depths of the sea. (Matthew 18:6) NIV

It would be better for him to

sit on the Dallas Cowboys sidelines and cheer for their opponent

be sent into the New York subway at midnight wearing expensive jewelry

to tease a Rottweiler

represent conservative views on "Donahue"

MOST-REQUESTED MIRACLES IN SOUTHERN CALIFORNIA CHURCHES

Parting rush-hour traffic on freeway

Rebuking of UV rays

The opportunity to direct feature films

Finding a plastic surgeon who's a Christian

Blessing your car with a decent parking space

Turning working waitresses into working actresses

Allowing home swept away by mudslide to stop at a more
    desirable location

Restoring hair

Cursing of cellulite

Turning tap water into Evian

Casting out of wrinkles

Getting a decent agent

Healing of San Andreas fault

HOW WE KNOW THE  BRADY BUNCH WEREN'T SPIRIT-FILLED CHRISTIANS

Marsha, Jan, and Cindy wore mini-skirts.

The kids constantly bet on stuff.

Greg once had a pack of cigarettes in his pocket.

The family never said grace at mealtime.

Cindy was a tattletale.

Questionable relationship between Alice and Sam the Butcher.

The kids didn't tithe allowances.

Although there was a houseful of people, apparently none were prayer partners.

There were recurrent occult images: the kids frequently dressed up as ghosts, and they believed the infamous Hawaiian tabu brought bad luck.

Mrs. Brady never asked the children, "How was your quiet time, dear?"

The entire family used euphemisms like "gosh," "gee," and "darn."

The older kids were allowed to attend dances.

Mr. and Mrs. Brady never attended Marriage Encounter weekends.

The Bradys' hit song "We Can Make the World a Whole Lot Better" never mentions Jesus.

Before purchasing a new car, cruise church parking lots to determine what vehicles are currently popular among the brethren. If possible, choose something with spiritual significance. (Honda made in-roads into Christendom several years ago with its unity-building model based on Acts 8:6, "the people with one *accord* gave heed.")

Realize that, with just a little customization, you can use your car as an "autowitness tool." Get a personalized license plate with "JN 3 16," "R U SAVD" or other testimony-oriented message on it which will complement your "Jesus is Lord" front license plate. Accessorize with as many bumper stickers ("In case of rapture, this vehicle will be unmanned") as possible. Place a school of fish symbols across your trunk. Hang a car deodorizer printed with a Bible verse from your rear-view mirror.

While driving, obey all safety rules and help others to do the same. If you see another car exceeding the speed limit in the fast lane, move into its lane and slow it down to the designated speed limit. Ignore the driver's horn-honking, light-flashing, and hand gestures, remembering the question from Psalm 2:1, "Why do the heathen rage?" Your actions may save the life of someone who hasn't yet made a profession of faith.

When stopped at a traffic light, roll down your windows and crank up your Bible teaching tape or Christian music and pray that you may "plant a seed" to the godless who may be stuck at your intersection. Although you may find yourself caught up in worship and desire to lift "holy hands," resist the urge; it makes the highway patrol suspicious and fellow drivers nervous.

Should you happen upon an accident, stop and quote Romans 8:28, "All things work together for good to them that love God" to the victims and police officers. If they look at you strangely, realize that they probably don't have ears to hear and drive on.

If you carpool with non-believers, make sure your conversation is as spiritual as possible. Work in numerous references to activities at your church. Mention that you heard someone say he heard about a large, nationally known company that was using all its profits for the devil.

Should you visit a friend or family member in the hospital, feel free to use the clergy parking space right next to the door. After all, your minister says that, based on 1 Peter 2:9, we are all priests.

Finally, should you get pulled over by a police officer, it's your responsibility to submit to authorities and to those who spitefully misuse you. Should being "a good Christian on your way to church" not get you out of the ticket and you are sent to court, remember not to worry because the Holy Spirit will "give you utterance."

A *love* offering still means you have to give money.

The "gulf" that separated the rich man and Lazarus did not become a BP.

The Great Commission is not a percentage.

It is not known if angels have wings but most First Baptist church buildings have several—usually named after rich deceased members.

As a young boy, Jesus did not have a halo of light around his head. If he had, he would have gotten caught a lot when playing "hide-and-seek."

TOPICS ON  FOR NATIONAL COUNCIL OF CHURCHES

Should Hulkamania Be Recognized As a Religion?

With Such A Religious Name, Wouldn't Madonna Make One
    Cool Spokesperson?

Wouldn't "I'm Okay, You're Okay" Be a Neat Motto?

Can Jesus' Teachings Be Made More Politically Correct?

Should the St. Louis Cardinals Be Allowed to Send a
  Representative?

Do We Know Anyone Who Could Get Michael Jackson to Sing
  "Heal The World" at the Annual Picnic?

Aren't Druids Kinda Like Christians?

How Come the U.N. Gets to Impose Sanctions And Order
  Bombing Strikes While We Just Do This Wimpy
  Humanitarian Stuff?

Resolved: People Who Do Bad Things Should Stop.

You Don't Have to Be Egyptian to Be in d'Nile

Stop the Bus! Riveting True-Life Tales from Youth Pastors

101 Crossword Puzzles for Slow Sermons

Cliff Notes on 2 John

Making 'Home School' Yearbooks More Interesting

Not Yet, Son: A Precursor to a Boy's First Reading of "Song
of Solomon"

Easy Things to Give Up for Lent

Multi-Level Marketing Made Easy with Your Church Directory

Charlton Heston's Bible Commentary

Transforming Your Home into a Parsonage for Tax Purposes

It Happened at the Church Where My Friend's Friend Went:
Undocumented Signs, Wonders, and Angel Sightings

This Pleasant Darkness: Maintaining a Positive Outlook in
Bad Situations

Did Noah include termites on the ark?

How could you be a good Jewish boy with a name like Ham?

What was God thinking when he created aardvarks?

Exactly where is *kingdom come* and have a lot of kids been
   sent there?

How can televangelists preach against the evils of incurring debt while allowing contributors to make pledges using Visa and MasterCard?

Why is the practice called *fasting* when time passes so slowly when you're doing it?

What does an atheist do when he drives up behind a car with a "Honk if you love Jesus" bumper sticker and that car doesn't move when the traffic light turns green?

How does God feel about radar detectors?

Is there biblical precedents for any of the following ideas being used by the contemporary church: gymnatoriums, visitor cards, offering envelopes, Christian music skate nights?

Not that it matters, but just how many angels really could dance on the head of a pin?

Why did Jesus ask people to follow and then believe, and we reverse that order?

Is "the place of quiet rest" mentioned in the Bible the Old Testament equivalent of a "time-out chair?"

HOT SEMINARS AT WOMEN'S CONFERENCES

"Organizing Your Prayer Closet"

"The Witness of Fitness"

"Christian Weight Loss—More of Jesus, Less of Me"

"Sewing and Reaping"

"Christian Cooking: When the Casserole Is Called Up Yonder, I'll Be There"

"Contentious" is "Content" Gone Too Far

Let Us Bake Bread Together

Tongue-Tied: Lassoing the Galloping Gossip

Showers of Blessing: Creating Better Prenuptial Parties

The Great Debate Over Heeling: Pumps vs. Flats

To Every Skin Tone There is a Season

Bow-Tying: Spiritual Gift or Learned Discipline

A GLOSSARY OF CHURCHSPEAK

affirmaniac—(af-fur-mane-ee-ak) person who has an uncontrollable habit of verbally agreeing with others' prayers, even before the thought is fully expressed:

FRIEND: God, today we want to. . .

AFFIRMANIAC: Yes, Lord! Yes, Lord!

FRIEND: . . . Pray for those who speak before they think.

AFFIRMANIAC: Yes, Lord!

altarcation—(awl-tur-kā-shun) violent disagreement with what the preacher has said from the pulpit.

altar ego—(awl-tur· ee-gō) clergy member who seems to be a regular guy if you meet him at the mall but undergoes a personality transformation after donning his or her vestments:

MALL GREETING: "Hey, how's it going?"

CHURCH GREETING: "Sister, how are you on this blessed Lord's Day?"

amenities—(a-men-uh-tees) things you pray for God to give you.

annoyted—(a-noi-ted) people irritated by the overuse of the word *anointed* to describe everything from sermons to aerobics classes.

apastacy—(a-pahst-ah-see) horror of having a potluck dinner without macaroni and cheese.

badolescent—(bad-ō-les-sent) notorious teenager in the church bent on proving that the seven deadly sins aren't so lethal.

baptician—(bap-ti-shun) stylist who immerses one's hair in the sink and raises it to new life with such consecrated coiffures as the Great Southern swoop, the deep-fried perm, and the agitated beehive.

Bathsheebiejeebies—(bath-shee-bee-jee-bees) involuntary shudder of a single man when he suddenly realizes the woman he is admiring is wearing a wedding band.

bendaddiction—(bend-ah-dik-shun) obsessive-compulsive belief that kneeling is the only way to get close to God.

black-and-white collar crime—(blak-and-whīt· kol-lur· krīm) priests accused of wrong-doing.

blarathon—(blayr-uh-thon) long, loud, and bombastic sermons by preachers who don't seem to understand the purpose of the public address system.

blestival—(bles-ti-vul) colossal event which includes big-name Christian musicians and, typically, Tony Campolo.

bodybuilder—(bŏ-dee-bil-dur) person preoccupied with increasing the size of the church, the capacity of the sanctuary, or other tangible signs of growth. His or her favorite part of the Bible is the Book of Numbers. To this person, there's nothing better than a Sunday school attendance drive.

boomering—(boo-muh-ring) shrill feedback which results from tapping the microphone to see if it's on.

bulldozer—(bul-dōz-ur) totally disinterested teenager who sees sermons as an excellent opportunity to catch a few z's.

cathedrawl—(kah-thee-drawl) mauling of liturgy by Southerners: e.g., Hey, ol' Mary, full of grays.

choiropractor—(kwirh-ō-prak-tor) physical therapist qualified to treat those in highly energetic choir injured by too much swaying.

cocodependent—(kō-kō-dē-pen-dent) person addicted to hot chocolate, generally a result of attending too many retreat afterglows.

conmissionary—(kon-mi-shun-air-ee) incarcerated Christian who evangelizes while in prison.

crosstify—(kros-ti-fī) compulsion of Christian organizations to turn all their t's in their names into crosses on stationery.

crummunion—(krum-mew-nyun) little bits of bread left in the plate after everyone has taken his pinch.

deparchment—(dē-parch-ment) getting up in the middle of the service to quench an agonizing thirst.

derangement—(dē-rainj-ment) choir members straying from pitch or parts that destroys a music director's hours of hard work.

disorganization—(dis-org-an-i-zā-shun) chaos which results when the choir and congregation mistake the organist's introduction for the beginning of the first verse.

doodleronomy—(doo-dul-rŏ-nō-mee) study of the scribblings left on the backs of attendance cards and offerings envelopes.

dormantory—(dor-mant-or-ee) church badly in need of a "wake-up call."

double-crossover—(dub-ul-krŏs-ō-vur) confusion of Christian artists finding acceptance in the musical mainstream and realizing that their songs "going into all the world" earn sour notes from angry Christian fans.

dysplexia—(dis-pleks-ee-uh) condition which results in placing transparencies backward or upside down on the overhead projector.

elevators—(el-uh-vā-torz) those who are miraculously delivered from addictions without working through 12-step programs.

engraven images—(en-grā-ven · i-maj-ez) little plaques that tell you who paid for the pews, stained glass, and statuary in the building.

estrogenesis—(es-trō-jen-uh-sis) study of how God used women through the ages. Weekend Estrogenesis seminars include opportunities for participants to be fearfully and wonderfully made-over.

eternilator—(ee-turn-i-lā-tor) big-name hired gun evangelist brought in to terrify the lost into the kingdom. The most unscrupulous sum up The Book of Revelation with the sentence, "He'll be-e-e ba-a-ack."

ethers—(ĕth-urz) people firmly committed to the King James Version of the Bible, who believeth that the Lord kneweth of which He spaketh when He didst spaketh thusly.

evangeletics—(ē-van-jah-let-iks) school of thinking that says church sports are the way to win lost but well-coordinated souls to Christ.

famble—(fam-bul) noisy scramble of family members trying to reunite when Sunday school is dismissed.

faith-to-sight-seers—(fāth-tū-sīt-see-urz) Holy Land tourists who finally visit the places they've always read about (although Peter and Andrew's Souvenir T-Shirt Shop probably wasn't around in the first century).

flyfishing—(flī-fish-ing) discretely checking to make sure your zipper is zipped without alerting others to your fear; practiced most by people seated on podiums facing the congregation.

Galileeria—(gă-lĭ-lee-ree-ah) retail mega-booths set up at Christian conferences offering everything from portable baptistries to spiritual warfare video games.

gigantuary—(jī-gan-chū-ayr-ee) megachurch worship center which is big enough to hold a three-ring circus and usually does.

gividends—(giv-uh-dindz) promised return on a tithe.

gomads—(gō-madz) people who wander from church to church: they go to one place till they get mad *and then* go *somewhere else. Also referred to as steeplechasers and leavangelicals.*

gosperity—(gō-spayr-uh-tee) doctrine that promotes materialism as a sign that you are truly among those God likes best.

gracier—(grā-shur) huddled mass of blue-haired widows trying to avoid frostbite when overzealous deacons crank up the air conditioning. Year-round you spot these women by looking for sweaters or sniffing for Woolite.

Greektomee—(greek-tū-mee) Christian organizations that use ancient words such as *koinonia, shekinah,* and *agape* that most people can't pronounce or understand.

Halloweenies—(hă-lō-ween-eez) those who take a soft stand on All Saints' Eve.

Hebrewsky—(hee-broo-skee) slang for ancient Jewish beer.

heirhead—(air-hĕd) person who believes that being a child of God exempts you from the trials of life. Confident that "he whom God blesses has no messes," heirheads are sure there must have been something wrong with the spiritual lives of Stephen, Paul, and Corrie ten Boom.

hemlock—(hĕm-lŏk) guideline which suggests the maximum shortness for skirts, generally used at Christian schools.

herewearz—(hear-wē-arz) missionary slide shows, which generally begin as follows: "Here we are at the airport." Click. "Here we are at the border." Click. "Here we are in the village." Click . . .

holy stroller—(hō-lee·strō-lur) man who tends to roam around the building throughout entire Sunday service. Although it seems this is his sanctioned responsibility, it's really just a way to avoid the sermon.

homemogenize—(hōm-ŏ-jah-nihz) repersonalization of a large church by breaking up into neighborhood home groups.

hormonastery—(hor-moan-uh-stayr-ee) singles groups which prove that "abstinence makes the heart grow fonder."

howaruzis—(how-ar-ū-zeez) rapid-fire hellos during the one-minute "greet-your-neighbor" periods in worship, which facilitates surface-to-surface conversations.

hymnasium—(him-nā-zee-um) church activities center where you can shoot hoops while Christian music blasts away.

hymnline—(him-line) the thin ribbon used to mark the place in the songbook.

hypeocrasy—(hip-ŏ-krah-see) radio spots promoting Christian rock concerts, marked by big booming voices with lots of reverb, claiming powerful effects the event will have on those who attend,

ANNOUNCER: They rattle the gates of hell and now they're coming to blast you into the kingdom of God. See "Scum No More," appearing live at the Born-Again Spirit-Filled Solid on the Rock Church this Saturday night!

ichthusiastic—(ik-thoos-ee-as-tik) being so excited about Jesus that you put Christian fish symbols on your checkbook, car, lapel, door, and children's notebooks.

incensitive—(in-sen-suh-tiv) predisposition to uncontrollable coughing caused by inhaling too many candle fumes or too much incense.

inspirographics—(in-spīr-ō-graf-iks) archaic drawings of praying hands, Easter lilies, church buses, and other sacred symbols used to spice up church bulletins.

isoulationism—(eye-soul-aye-shun-ism) tendency to associate exclusively with other Christians.

jellofy—(jĕl-ō-fī) tendency for a small group of interlocked people to sway, shake, and ripple during heavily emotional worship services.

jezebellion—(jez-uh-bel-yun) uprising in the church caused by a woman more intent on making waves than testing the waters.

justification—(just-if-ĭ-kā-shun) frequent and sometimes irritating insertion of the word *just* into prayers to make talking to God seem more conversational or humble. "Father God, we just want to just thank You for being just so loving and just so just."

Later Day Saints—(lay-tur·dā·sants) people who tend to arrive sometime after the service begins.

locustard—(lō-kŭs-terd) creative and healthy dessert invented by John the Baptist.

mammonaries—(mam-mon-ayhr-ees) wealthy church people whose vocation is to bankroll mission trips and other events requiring large amounts of money.

mercynary—(mur-see-nayhr-ee) person vigilant in taking up the causes of the downtrodden, forgotten, and hurting.

Methusalization—(meh-thoos-uh-luh-zā-shun) aging of a congregation. A sure sign of this process: nursery converted to an arts-and-crafts center.

minor profits—(mi-ner pro-fits) pocket change made at exhausting junior high bake sale.

mintistry—(mint-i-tree) service provided by the person who always brings Lifesavers or TicTacs to church to cure people of dreaded "worship breath."

mystery prayer—(mis-tur-ee prayr) petition for unspoken request. As a public service, some churches offer this generic multipurpose prayer:
God, we pray for this brother/sister, that whatever he/she did or didn't do, has or doesn't have, wants or doesn't want. Whatever it is, we pray forgiveness, healing, conviction, blessing, comfort, or provision. Raise them up, bring them

down, or restore them. In all things, we ask that Thy will be done. Amen.

napology—(nap-ŏ-lŏ-gee) assistant pastor's verbal restitution in the Monday morning staff meeting after dozing off during the senior pastor's sermon.

nodfellows—(nŏd-fel-ōz) men who fall asleep during worship services.

the numb and the restless—(thu· nuhm ·and·thu ·rest-les) youth section of the church, who vascillate between snoozing and squirming.

oftenatory hymn—(off-en-ah-tor-ee ·him) song used so frequently that it becomes the scourge of the congregation.

onoyadont—(oh-nō-ya-dōnt) youth pastor's "sex talk," strongly advocating celibacy until marriage.

orderination—(or-der-in-nā-shun) zealous maintenance of the Order of Service; would not be change if Christ Himself returned.

parsonality test—(par-sun-al-uh-tee·test) diagnostic tool to evaluate ministerial candidates.

palmenade—(pahlm-in-ād) high-falooting processional used in Easter pageants, depicting Jesus' triumphant entry into Jerusalem.

pastorized—(pas-tur-eyezd) post-service routine comprised of being greeted by preacher, quickly shaking his hand, and offering him a standardized compliment of the sermon.

pewtrid—(pew-trid) dried-up chewing gum and other ancient artifacts found under the seats in the sanctuary.

pewtrified—(pew-tri-fīd) 1) dead church which wouldn't be on fire if you napalmed them; 2) being overtaken with numbness in the posterior after sitting too long in church.

prayer worrier—(prayr·wur-ree-ur) unlike the prayer warrior, who seems to know God's heart, this person feels he or she must read books, listen to tapes, or attend conferences before he or she will know how to talk to God properly.

prayerority—(prayr-or-uh-tee) what a person believes is "on God's heart" when it's time to talk to Him.

puddle huddle—(pud-dul·hud-dul) emotionally overwrought, intertwined, cluster of teenagers; generally forms on the last night of church camp.

pulpitation—(pul-pi-tā-shun) rapid beat of a parishioner's heart when "Just As I Am" is being played through for the third time and the preacher is begging for sinners to delay no longer.

rapostolic ministry—(rap-ō-stol-ik·min-is-tree) musicians who lay down the Gospel to a hiphop beat: Logos to your mother.

recumenical—(rek-yū-men-uh-kul) opening of church league sports to people of all faiths.

reformation—(re-form-ā-shun) what parents hope will happen to their delinquent teenagers in Bible study classes.

ricosharing—(rik-ō-shayr-eeng) preacher's object lessons which are given during children's church, but are intended to bounce over their heads and score bullseyes with the adults.

rollerkoshers—(rōl-lur·kō-sherz) members of charismatic Messianic fellowships known for their polka-like song and dance routines.

salivagation—(sa-li-vuh-gā-shun) licking of fingertips necessary to turn the thin parchment pages of a Bible.

schismy seeds—(siz-um-ee·seedz) gossip, half-truths, and hearsay that plant division in a church.

self-centers—(self-sen-turz) section in bookstores that tells you how to accomplish almost anything without having to interact with others.

sermonex—(sur-mon-eks) preacher's message guaranteed to put the congregation to sleep.

shoulder holder—(shōl-dur·hōl-dur) one who tends to hug members of opposite sex from the side in order to avoid excessive torso touching.

sigh language—(sī·lang-wej) joint exhaling which communicates, "We're about to enter into a group prayer."

sinktification—(sink-ti-fuh-kā-shun) prayer uttered by a church league basketball player before shooting a free throw.

sinsation—(sin-sā-shun) press hype about a wrongdoing by a prominent religious leader.

sistren—(sis-tren) female equivalent of brethren; Sensitive to exclusive language, the preferred usage by Methodists is simply the neutral term of "ren."

smoke ring—(smōk·ring) a circle of people (usually comprised of deacons) who puff cigarettes between Sunday school and worship services.

smusher—(smush-ur) overzealous usher determined to cram at least three more people into your already packed row.

spiellunking—(speel-lunk-ing) minister's verbal wandering "in the dark" until he finds his way from a tangent back to the point he was trying to make.

spliturgy—(split-ur-jee) congregational reading which falls out of unison and deteriorates into a syncopated mumble.

Spittite—-(spit-tīt) person on the front row who is showered by preachers tending to spray when they speak. Watch out if you're up front when they begin talking about "the apostle Peter preaching powerfully on Pentecost."

tapeworms—(tāp-wurmz) people who live for the next "anointed teaching" cassette that promises to change their lives.

tearorist—(tier-or-est) kid at church camp's open mike night who sparks uncontrollable emotion in motion while thanking everyone for making it such a great time. For maximum effectiveness, the tearorist requests Michael W. Smith's song "Friends," then says:

I just want to say (*sob, sob*) that I love you guys and (*gasp, gasp*) you're all my best friends and I'm going to write each (*sob, gasp, sob*) and every one of you every day for the rest of my life.

(For the typical crowd response, see *puddle huddle*.)

tensus—(ten-sus) a contracted form of tentative census, a technique frequently used by preachers who ask a question such as, "How many here believe in God's power?" and the congregation are unsure if they are supposed to raise their hands or not.

testostimony—(tes-taus-tuh-mō-nē) popularized by FCA, this is a brief conversion story of a male who becomes a Christian and moves from third-string benchwarmer to first-round draft choice in professional sports.

timexodus—(tym-eks-ō-dus) mass exit from church by those who closely watch their watches for the time it seems the preacher should cease-fire and let the parshioners go. In wealthy churches, this is known as "rolexodus."

titheton—(tīth-tun) financial giving of a megachurch, which generally has a building plan rivalling EPCOT.

tongue twisters—(tung·twis-turz) those who wrongly interpret the words of someone speaking in tongues.

tracknowledge—(trak-nahl-ij) ability to recite from memory the text of such brochures as Campus Crusade's "Four Spiritual Laws."

transverse—(trans-vurs) the stanza (usually the third) in a hymn that always gets skipped.

tri-blester—(trī-bles-tur) the triple backslap hug used by men in the church to show affection.

viddeists—(vid-dee-usts) those devoted folks who put their faith in God and television ministries (which never seems to have enough financing); these people are sometimes referred to as brainwatched.

wackolyte—(wak-ō-līt) a loose-cannon choir boy or girl known for unpredictable and often irreverent behavior.

waspnest—(wahsp-nest) church sheltered in safe yuppie neighborhood where members can delight in homogenity.

welcombers—(wel-cohm-urz) those friendly folks who prowl their neighborhoods, social clubs, and workplaces, scouting for potential new parishioners.

whinery—(whīn-ur-ee) child care supervisors' slang name for nursery.

 TITLES FOR THIS BOOK

You Can't Put a Square Pagan in a Round Hole

Sunday Funnies

Blessed Be the Tithe that Binds

Thee-Saurus

Holy Terrors and Loose Canons

Tower of Babbling-On

A Sunday with Nuts

Praise the Lord and Pass the Admonition